To Jan

One of the nicest persons

I've ever met,

Many Blessings,

Brenda

Granted A Second Chance To Say This

Brenda Carter-Foster

WESTBOW
PRESS
A DIVISION OF THOMAS NELSON

WestBow Press books may be ordered through booksellers or by contacting:

WestBow Press
A Division of Thomas Nelson
1663 Liberty Drive
Bloomington, IN 47403
www.westbowpress.com
1-(866) 928-1240

ISBN: 978-1-4497-2272-2 (sc)
ISBN: 978-1-4497-2426-9 (hc)
ISBN: 978-1-4497-2273-9 (e)

Library of Congress Control Number: 2011914741

Printed in the United States of America

WestBow Press rev. date: 11/17/2011

About the Author

Married to Robert Foster, we have four children, two daughters Sean and Khandi and two sons Vincent and Kenneth, Grandchildren and Great Grand Children. I currently work for the Massachusetts Court System in the Information Technology Department.

About the Book

Writing about my thoughts and experiences in the form of poetry.

Prologue

Who asks to be homeless? I did not, but it happened to me. I left Baltimore to come to Massachusetts to work as a welder at the Quincy Shipyard. I wanted to make a better life for my family and I. I had been laid off as a welder at the Sparrows Point Shipyard and was working as a maid at the Howard Johnson's Hotel when a recruiter for Quincy Shipyard approached me and asked if I knew of any laid off shipyard workers looking for work. I told him that I was a welder and was interested. He asked me to take a welding test and then I was hired. The living conditions that he told me and the men and women that I referred to him were lies. He had a hotel room with two beds, for more than a dozen women who were recruited from different states to stay. I slept on the floor and left in the morning looking for a room. I could not afford the cost for a room at the hotel. I slept from pillar to post and had to leave some places in the middle of the night and before dawn because somebody's husband or boyfriend would try to take advantage of me because I was alone. Wrong. I slept at Greyhound, Trailways Bus Stations, and Amtrak Train Station. I also rented a room, in a men's boarding house and slept in vestibules. I left one place because a lady's boyfriend was standing over me while I was sleeping on a sofa. I left that night with no place to go. Walking and crying in the rain, I was approached by a man who asked me what was wrong. I told him that I was looking for a room to rent. He was just another stranger like everyone else that I had encountered previously. By now I was mentally and physically drained and being naive. He said I think Ms. (can not remember her given name) gotta a room. I walked upstairs to what looked like a rooming house to me. I stepped inside to where she was supposed to be.

He started locking and kept locking the door, there were about four or five locks on the door. It was an efficiency apartment, he backed me into the bedroom into a chair as he sat on the bed and pulled a shotgun from under the mattress and said give me a kiss honey. I could not and I would not kiss him. He asked me again what was my name and I told him Brenda. He broke down and started crying and apologized saying that he had a daughter named Brenda. I sat in the chair all night and eventually, I fell asleep. He left bags of groceries and a note on the kitchen table apologizing again. The note read, that I could stay if I wanted to. I left out of there flying and never looked back. After what had just happened to me made me realize that God had taken all the fear from me which kept me from getting shot and possibly murdered. God was totally in control of my situation for which I am eternally grateful. My family and friends encouraged me to write a book of poetry. If I can give back by writing and giving to the homeless I will never cease to keep on writing. I decided that all proceeds from this book will be donated to the homeless. If you have been fortunate and never experienced being homeless you have no idea what a person endures. I want to praise God in my poetry and give thanks for all that He has brought me through.

The start of me writing poetry again, came about when I took a bible study class at my church, Mount Moriah Baptist Church. Our class was instructed to write a Psalm in our own words.

Remembering Psalm

Upwards I stretch my hands to thee. Father hear my

plea.

I ask forgiveness in my Sinful ways.

When I did not call on you who saved me from my

enemies

Who Smiled and kissed me on the cheek

And slandered my name day and night.

You Brought me back from darkness and illuminated

my way.

From the restless and Unfulfilled life to joy and

learning the Word.

I could not see before you gave me insight beyond my

pain.

A cruel and cold world waiting to devour me.
Feeling Despair until your impartation of love lifted me to higher ground.

PRAISE HIM.

I ran from pillar to post for a very long time until I found a safe place to live. I never thought I would experience what it is like to be homeless. People look at you with angry eyes not knowing or caring about your situation. Because of God's grace and mercy, I no longer have to endure such indignities.

Homeless

I walked the streets after being chased

From many places where I laid my head.

Even though my rent for my room was always paid.

I was alone and therefore thought of as an easy prey.

I slept on floors, couches, in vestibules, standing and

sleepwalking.

God was watching over me all the time for whom I

could never repay.

I was trying to find my way in the world all by myself.

How foolish Of me to think that I did not need His

help.

I was sick and tired of being so disappointed. I was

turned down

For half-way decent apartments that I wanted

But could not afford the cost. Worn out and feeling
very lost.

God was pushing me every day when I felt like
giving up.

All of the bad experiences that I had encountered,
God was there to pick me up. I came in contact with
many people

Sleeping on the streets. So much cruelty is inflicted
on the homeless

and they are so easy to mistreat. God let me go through
this to

Witness first hand that we all could make a stand and
help our fellowman.

This poem is about how I feel inside and can never really write or speak about how thankful I am that I no longer have to endure such indignities.

Pure Thanks

Father, to you be the glory

For only you know the whole story.

My life was not to me worth living

Had you not been so forgiving.

You spared my life countless times,

I stretch my hands up to you with praise.

From this day on and always,

When I was alone and felt despair

No else was there.

Then, I did not realize the love you showered on my soul.

I could not return love for I was angry and cold.

Bent on self-destruction until your re-construction of

my life

Reminded me of the toil and strife,

And how you paid the ultimate price.

I feel especially blessed to have my mother who loves, laughs, prays, encourages and uplifts the family at **all** times.

Blessed With Bess

Bessie is my mom, she is full of charm,

Her beautiful smile does no harm. Standing five feet

tall.

Oops in her mind five feet two. What can I say? I must

Agree, I do not need that woman after me.

She is a senior citizen with the zest of a woman

Twice her junior. A heart of pure gold. Everybody

Knows Ms. Bessie. She will lend a hand whenever

Needed. Children run to her and can not wait to greet

her.

They know a loving touch can never be too much.

Bessie raised my two sisters and two others my

Brothers who had to watch westerns, war movies

And to match their personalities the Stooges.

Mom would let us share the TV and when that

could not

Work she told us stories about our roots with wit and

Humor. My mom is the "best"—it is not just a rumor.

On Tuesday night at my church we show up and show out giving praise to the Lord.

Tuesday Night Prayer

Praising the Lord is how we get the blessings to flow.

The love in this place is all a glow.

The hugs and embraces are for all the races.

Color is never a factor or an excuse to show abuse.

We pray to be stronger and wiser to do the Lord's will.

The scriptures we hold close to our hearts and try

to fulfill.

When we see a Sister or Brother fall down,

Do not run and attack like you have all the power.

One's life is like a delicate flower.

Pray for a speedy recovery that this person will not

feel like a disgrace.

One who can stand and show their face.

A smile, a hug, a prayer or even a dollar will do so

much to inspire.

This person is not a failure—Just fell down.

Let me tell you about my grandson Anthony Bonnett. He is the best grandson I could ever hope for. Obedient, smart, honest, handsome, happy, loving, caring, hard working and can sometimes be a pain when his joking is endless. Nothing makes me happier than to see him full of life.

A Prayer For My Grandson

My grandson Anthony is the light of my world.

He will laugh and play, makes my Head swirl.

No longer is he the little boy who filled my heart with

joy.

Now he is a Teenager who I pray will follow the plan

of the Master.

Young boys want to grow Up fast, fast and faster.

Not realizing the pressures of the world.

Cold hard facts Of pain he will endure.

There will be things to him that I cannot explain.

I do not Have all the answers, all I can teach

My grandson is to always pray.

I am very proud of my daughters Sean and Khandi. Vincent and Kenneth are my stepsons whom I love. I could not have had better stepsons. I have the responsibility of being a mother and to be the best that I know how to be.

My beautiful friend Claudette Blot a mighty Woman of God asked me to write a poem for our church on Mother's Day.

Precious Mothers

A mother's first look at her child is with joy and a

smile.

Thanking God for the gift he entrusted her with.

The tears flow naturally because she is so overjoyed.

From mom exudes everlasting love.

The peace between Mother and child is like that of a

dove.

There is also another kind of Mother.

One who did not give birth, but raised a child with

loving girth.

She too, is also grateful to God for whatever

Circumstances placed this child in her care.

She also made sacrifices without the fanfare.

A mother raises her child to show respect for God

And others. Mothers will not let their child

disrespect others as a joke.

We love our mothers no matter what, even after we

have verbally fought.

When we disobey what a price we pay.

All because we did not want to hear what Momma

said.

Now, I have to face mom and say thank you for

loving me.

I really did not mean to doubt you, I just could not

see.

Mom leans over and gives me a hug.

She says Thank you Lord for my child.

So even if your mother is not present with you now,

Picture her face and see her smile. Mothers are

lifesavers

Who never wear down. They go to heaven for putting

up with us

To receive their crown. Happy Mothers' Day Mom.

After watching the Democratic and Republican Conventions when it was over I came up with this.

W O W
ipe ut ar

The reality of insanity involves humanity.

Our sons and daughters are sent to war with good

intentions

After the Democratic and Republican Conventions.

They've told us that the world cannot operate without

our involvement.

Let's do something about the homelessness, how

about building

Affordable developments. Our future generations go

to far off places

To see pain and suffering on the faces of people like

you and me.

Doing all they can to stay alive. War torn countries

and

Families torn apart over lies about oil and when

religion is used.

But if the truth is to be told—it is no excuse when we

are to

Love one another as our Brother.

My father was not a church going man but he believed in God. The conversations we had let me know that he loved me and gave me the best advice he knew.

My Dad

My dad I do adore

We shared talks and fun galore.

He taught me right from wrong.

I miss him so much now that he is gone.

I could tell him all my worries.

He would give the best advice, because he was so

wise.

Tell the truth child

You have no need to lie

Trust in the Lord and talk to him whenever you want to.

Carry not a heavy burden He will see you through.

That is what my dad told me to do.

I am so thankful to the Lord

My dad and I are on one accord.

Happy Father's Day.

I really believe in my heart that Barack Hussein Obama was chosen to be one of the leaders of the world to unite countries worldwide in peace.

Change

A change we said is what we need

But how many of us can believe

The change we received? I am talking

About our first Black President, "Barack Hussein Obama"

Whom I believe was not chosen by man.

When God makes the changes that we pray for

It will be in His time and not before.

Hope restored for the world to see.

A man of color was the president to be.

Help someone you see that is in need.

Think twice for the choices that will make

The changes for you to fail or succeed.

Keep God in your life

There is no limitations to who you can be.

I have two sisters Trish (Patricia Carter) and Kneecee (Barbara Carter) we have been through it all. Arguing, fighting, laughing, hugging, screaming at one another. The bottom line is, we love one another and nothing can separate our love.

Sister's Anger

We have shared the bed, food, clothes and everything

else.

Because we love one another, we never kept it all for self.

From children to grown up folks, we laughed, argued

And cried. Never once wanted the other to die. In each

Other's presence unspoken anger resides. The smile is

No longer in the eyes. One says the other is wrong.

Explanation unacceptable just wrong. We need to come

To an agreement on this forever relationship before a

fatal

Hate trip. One has to step up to the plate before it is

too late.

Prayers must be said to put this pain on the mend.

So that we can pick up as though it never began. Still I

Will always love you even when you are wrong.

Real friendship is priceless.

Hazel

This friend of mine, Hazel is her name.

She helps those in need and reveals her past.

Condemns no one or has a stone to cast.

She tells of her trial and tribulations when asked.

It is said without trepidation. She enlightens and prays

For the down trodden, no one is left out or forgotten.

A gift she has of intuition, advises when asked for an

opinion.

Maybe it is not what you wanted to hear. The truth is

spoken and it is crystal clear.

It is good to have a friend who is there for you. No

matter

What you are going through. Prayer is her main focus

to get things on

The move and done. After business is taken care of

she involves all

To celebrate and have fun. A friend to me is more

precious

Than diamonds and gold. No Price can be put on

true friendship

To be sold. Hazel Stanton is a Sistah's Sister.

I wonder what a soldier would think if he is in this position.

Why Fear

God has sent an angel to watch over me.

I dare to fear what I cannot see.

Moving about in this war I did not ask for.

Searching for the enemy.

Who looks like me, this bombed out place

That looks to be deserted.

Hearing noises and seeing shadows

Makes me feel disconcerted.

I must not weaken in my belief.

That God has sent an angel to watch over me.

That sound I hear of a baby's cry.

Freezes our movement in time.

Our hearts are heavy to hear an innocent sigh.

The sergeant signals us to

Invade but before we tried

The mother appears with her babe

And looks into our eyes. Another step

We would have been, booby-trapped.

God sent two angels to watch over us.

A platoon of men saved by the enemy.

They were angels watching over us.

She asked me to write a poem for her graduation.

There Are No Exceptions

From the streets of pain her journey began
Battling foes, drugs and shame. Doing everything
To rid the pain. So many times she tried to ignore
The calling, running scared, stumbling and falling.
She said, Lord hear my plea. I know I am not worth
It to any degree. The Lord again said to her Coralotta
I love you too my child. Come in from the ways of the
World. There is nothing you can do out there, it is all
Despair. She took heed and planted the seed out of
Gratefulness forever changing her life. She thanked the
Lord countless times and said never again will I whine.
I want to teach about your love, kindness,
understanding
and forgiveness. I will teach and spread your word for
All to hear. Let them know about your loving care.

So the Lord granted Coralotta with the gift to teach
And an anointing to preach. She thought she was not
Worth a dime. The Lord cleaned her up and renewed
Her mind. The learning, the classes and the degree.
None of this she could foresee. Only the Lord knows
What is in store for each of us when we believe and
give Him our trust. Congratulations Rev. Dr. Coralotta
Darwin Bates for all you have achieved. This was all
Made possible because in the Lord you believed.

Do you know this boy?

Hard Headed Boy

You get with this bad boy who lives on the street.

You are trying to impress him for A friend you

mistreat.

Your buddy you've been with since third grade.

His feelings You hurt by trying to degrade. In your heart

you

Know you are wrong. You sing with your new friend

your

Old pals favorite song. In his eyes you see the hurt

Where it use to be content. Your new friend was kicked

out of

His home because When mom left for work he would

leave his

Younger siblings alone. She asked him why does he

leave them

And stay. He raised his hand at mom to inflict fear.

Dead wrong son.

Mom called the ambulance and prayed for his

recovery.

While he was recuperating in his discovery he new

never

Again will he disrespect mom.

I wrote this about a woman who takes in children after she has raised her own.

An Angel Among Us

Olga is one of the first faces that I am use to seeing.

At prayer services, Touching and agreeing.

She prays from the heart in a soft clear voice.

When you know that you know is usually her start.

After that it is all powerful.

Lifting up the sick, jobless, homeless in Jesus' name.

The love is all the same.

She reaches out to a child and shows

Much love and support with a smile.

She never complains or demands.

Olga is a warrior who obeys

Christ's commands. Contributing, advising, arranging,

Supplying and resolving. Involved with church plans

To do whatever she can.

An angel walks among us.

Olga Mancortes is her Name.

This teenage girl can not wait to celebrate her sixteenth birthday arriving into womanhood.

Little Sister

Hey girl, it is good to see you again. You are looking
fresh and sweet.

How have you been? I know you just did not curse
like a sailor.

Do not you dare repeat. You just turned sixteen you
are a teenage queen.

Do not go all out to be seen. You were not raised to
act like that. Mom and Nana

Raised you in church and sent you to school. Slow
down child

Do not act like that is cool. I am not fussing at you
doll only trying to show you.

Your girls are hanging out your top and your skirt is
showing ole glory.

Boys are whistling at you because they think you
have not been taught or shown.
Bring it up a notch girl. Laugh, have fun and let it be
known
That you are a child of the King. Do not act like a bad
girl trying to fit in.
Choose your friends wisely, for you will be judged by
the company you keep.
Stay on the path to obtain your goals. You can make it
to the top
Without losing your soul.

To open my eyes and rise is a lot to be grateful for.

Awakening

As I awake in my bed, thank you Lord needs to be
said.

I could have been lying In my grave.

Time and time again my life you saved.

Traveling on the highway of life,

I take notice to the sunlight from trees,

Opened windows and feeling the cool breeze.

How thankful to say that

Because of you Lord I am here

Exists no longer the fear. It is been said

I've cheated death and all of that.

You saved me from the crashes, slashes,

Bullets and bats and all of life's threatening attacks.

So here I stand before you,

To let them know that only with God you will grow.

She is always the same, welcoming and smiling.

See Sister Jane Dance

She moves by the spirit in a holy trance
Look how Sis Jane can dance.
She swings and prances to worship the
Lord. Continuously praising our God.
She moves like the thunder the African
Queen that she is. She praises God in such
A free flowing spirit. Sis Jane dances so
Beautifully you cant keep still. You are
Thinking its so infectious it must be
God's will. Sis Jane blesses us with
Her smile. Dancing and praying all
The while. To see in flight her feet you can
Hear the African drum beat. To see her dance
Is really a treat before you know it you are
Out of your seat. Sis Jane Hendrickson
Keep blessing the Lord Sister.

We have all passed the homeless on the streets. How we look at them is with mixed emotions. Some people care, some with pity, some with hatred and some with love.

Looks Deceiving

This human being we pass on the street

Hair matted, clothes wrinkled and torn.

He is not made of glass or metal he was born.

Do we reach out or touch or give a quarter

Or say a prayer for this soul? Or do we leave

This body for slaughter? That is not my dad

Or my brother. Do we know who this really

Could be or do we really care? He is not getting

My change—why should I care? What if you

Look into the eyes of the soul? Lo and behold

The voice speaks so that only you can hear. You

Pass me by like wind strewn trash. How I got here

Is a long story of mankind and sad. You judge me

Thinking I must have been bad. Judge not—for you

Know not who this may be.

Good and bad relationships that we all can encounter
from time to time.

No Communication

The arguing and fussing, and fighting will not cease.

It is so out of hand you've had to involve the police.

You stand before the law in a black robe.

Your personal business in front of others

Is disclosed. It gets deeper than that when

Your life is probed. You stand there with a heartache

Saying, how did we get to this place.

Here comes the part that you dread to hear.

You must return on a later date to resolve

This issue and clear the air.

You two look at each other and just stare.

No words can repair the pain felt.

So you wrestle the hurt and despair.

The only way to get through this is with prayer.

You cry out to the Lord with the pain you feel.

Believe and trust that he will erase your fears.

You will began wiping away the tears.

Give him over to the Lord and take back.

Your life that was given to you to live abundantly and

free.

Sometimes a friendship may end in an instant. Sometimes it can start over.

Friend For Real

The eyes say hello and lips greet with a smile.

The face of one I have not seen in a while.

It seems like yesterday that we would.

Laugh and chatter regardless of the matter.

All of a sudden the eyes looks like daggers,

The smile a smirk. I think what a jerk.

No laughter just a chill, if looks could kill.

We call each other a friend,

Between us not even a grin what a sin.

It is hard when eye contact is not.

Easy to get back. A real friend will pick up

The slack and regain the friendship back.

To harden one's heart will keep us apart.

I tend to think when God gives us a friend.

We should share the joy and pain

Of each other's life until the end. So, I reach out

To you my friend. Let's be friends again . . . hello.

When we see each other in church Sunday after Sunday

it is okay to speak.

Speak Why Not

It is Sunday morning sitting in the pews praising God.

I look to my neighbor to say good morning how are

you?

They turn away and frown, as if I were about to

attack.

All I wanted to do was greet. I do not feel a defeat. I

came to

Worship not a twelve round bout. It is ok to smile and

greet

A member of our church family, as we are supposed

to do.

How would you feel if this happened to you? Turning to

the left

or right just to avoid speaking, You are missing

blessings

That you should be seeking. Do not enter Church with

an irascible behavior.

This is totally disrespectful to our Savior. No one has

the authority

To snub another, a smile or nod will suffice. Keep in

mind

We're sisters and brothers in Christ.

Having the Fatty Tumor removed from my arm was the last thing I wanted, but the pain was too much.

Fear or Faith

Ouuccch! my arm hurts as the night was creeping,

I am stretched out sleeping. Again, I repeat the same

thing

Only louder because of the pain. I sit up in my bed

feeling

So afraid that I only think the worse. I was picturing

myself

Like the one arm bandit. Then reality sits in and

makes me

Realize the Devil is a liar. I started praying for relief and

the fear

Was gone and the pain was gone. My faith replaced the

picture

Of doom and gloom. I thought I had the faith of a

mustard seed.

I weakened when I did not seek the Lord's help first. I automatically

Let fear take over and it almost ruined my night. Once I began

To pray and believe that God will not delay the healing.

Faith is second to nothing, so step up to the plate to activate.

He is listening.

When you are feeling out of sorts.

Why On Empty?

If you are feeling empty and blue

And do not know what to do

Give thanks for when you are having

A feeling that is not too appealing.

But after all you are above ground.

Come on you can remove that frown

Just like you did when Uncle Frank

Was acting like a clown, he fell down

The steps and you thought he was dead.

He did not make a sound,

The curtains and drapes covered his head.

You started going to church and all.

Give thanks. Remember when we did not have all the

rent

Short by $58.28 cents. Here comes the Sheriff

A posse ready to set us out

You started praying and out came a shout.

They had the wrong name on the

Eviction notice. Give thanks.

It is a time to laugh, cry, to be

Born and die. No matter the season

To give thanks is the reason to be

Blessed in ways seen and unseen.

Give thanks. On empty why?

Let the pat on the back be sincere.

In Sheep's Clothing

The pat on the back is not always good

Let that be understood

Be careful that the smile is not followed

By an attack

To say I am blessed, you are blessed

Why say it if you do not mean it?

Why not put it to the test?

The exchange of pleasantries is strained

A blessing to one another should try

To be gained.

WOW, I do not feel like I am in church

It should be a feeling of peace not hurt

So when I leave here today

I'll kneel and say

Lord teach us how to pray.

There is no time like the present.

The Time Is Now

We are truly living in challenging times.

Good news is seldom heard.

It seems to be always about crime.

We're not going to accept this bad news all the time,

Because we have Jesus on the mainline.

Keep your head up, knees down

And pray to God for a better way.

Our children are running wild and going astray.

Our children are enticed by worldly goods.

But to obtain them they turn to the corrupted.

Trying to affiliate with thugs.

Due to home life where they feel no love.

The streets will gladly be the babysitter.

Watching their pockets fill with cheddar.

Angie cursed her fifth grade teacher and has to stay
late.
Mom is home screaming.
Angie is always making me late for my dates.
Three year old Little Lenny is hungry and crying,
Ma do not leave peas. Dad's running out the door to
Pick up his honey they have tickets to sail.
Dad is saying, I owe this to myself, since I've been in
jail.
A perfect family does not exist.
Love, respect and prayers must we insist.
We cannot afford to blame the child
And any excuse they'll use to run wild.
Keep all families in your prayers tonight
So that no member takes flight.
And be blessed with the Jesus light.

Granted A Second Chance

My Thank You

First, I want to give Honor and Glory to God, for allowing me the privilege of writing this book. A special thank you to my Mother (Bessie) and my Husband (Robert) for all their love, encouragement and support. Also to my Children (Sean & Khandi), Grand Children (Sierra & Anthony), Sisters (Patricia & Kneecee) Brothers (Rev. E. A. Carter & William) & my co-workers (Sharon Neal, Beverly Lucas, Hazel Stanton, Evelyn Snow, Maritza Bond and Sandra Jenkins.

Last but not least, a great thank you to my Pastor Rev. Eugene Neville and Minister Ruth Neville, my church family and my Tuesday Night Prayer Team for their prayers and support. For all my other family members and friends, too many to be mentioned, thank you for showing me love and encouragement through out the years. To my typist Bev Lucas, many thanks for your patience and assistance in helping to make this book come together.

Greatly appreciated! God Bless all of you! With Love, Brenda Carter-Foster, Author. After reading this book, if you were touched by it and would like to experience the Joy of the Lord, I encourage you to invite Jesus into your heart today. Here are 3 reasons why you need Jesus. Because you have a past. You cannot go back, but He can. The Bible says, Jesus Christ is the same yesterday, today, and forever. (Hebrews 13:8). He can walk into those places of sin and failure, wipe the slate clean, and give you a new beginning. Because you need a friend. Jesus knows the worst about you, yet He believes the best. Why? Because He sees you not as you are, but as you will be when He gets through with you. What a friend! Because He holds the future. Are you going to trust Him? In His hands you are safe and secure—

today, tomorrow and for all eternity. His Words says, "For I know the plans I have for you . . . plans for good and not for evil, to give you a future and a hope. (Jeremiah 29:11-12).

If you will like to begin a personal relationship with Jesus today,

please pray this prayer:

Dear Lord Jesus, I know that I am a sinner, and I am asking for Your forgiveness. I believe that You died for my sins and rose from the dead. I turn from my sins and invite You to come into my heart and live. I want to trust and follow You as my Lord and Savior. In Jesus name I Pray. Amen."

CPSIA information can be obtained at www.ICGtesting.com
Printed in the USA
BVOW070221260112

281357BV00001B/4/P